FRIEDMUT WILHELM

The SUMMIT

A call for a Charter of Love and Compassion

authorHOUSE®

AuthorHouse™
1663 Liberty Drive
Bloomington, IN 47403
www.authorhouse.com
Phone: 1-800-839-8640

Published by AuthorHouse 2/13/2013

ISBN: 978-1-4817-1593-5 (sc)
ISBN: 978-1-4817-1591-1 (e)

Library of Congress Control Number: 2013902653

Any people depicted in stock imagery provided by Thinkstock are models,
and such images are being used for illustrative purposes only.
Certain stock imagery © Thinkstock.

This book is printed on acid-free paper.

To
L u c y
The Grand Mother of Mankind

*Once the truth has manifested itself
in a single mind, it will become a
force that sets everything on fire,
and nothing can stop it.*

Pierre Teilhard de Chardin

Table of Contents

Acknowledgements vii
In lieu of a foreword xiii
   Dear Professor E.O. Wilson   xiii
CHAPTER 1 1
   It's a WONDERFUL WORLD   1
CHAPTER 2 5
   DEFINING MOMENTS   5
   The MAN in the DARK SUIT   5
   The MAKING of ARMAGEDDON   15
   Conclusion   23
CHAPTER 3 27
   LUCY   27
CHAPTER 4 35
   HUNTERS and GATHERERS UNLIMITED   35
CHAPTER 5 47
   THE WEIRDNESS OF MAN and his
      GOODNESS   47
CHAPTER 6 59
   ATTEMPTS OF A CURE – A
      DISCUSSION ON THE RIDGE   60
   Biophilia   60
   Concept of education   61

The call on the Pastor   64

CHAPTER 7 67

  IDEAS   67

  THE AVALANCHE CHUTE AND
    THE CHARTER OF LOVE AND
    COMPASSION   68

  THE CLEARING IN THE FOREST AND
    THE NEW CHARTER SCHOOLS   74

  STATEMENT OF PURPOSE   75

  WHY DO WE NEED A NEW CHARTER   77

MANIFESTO..81

Post Script 85

  The Man in the Dark Suit – "Where are we
    going"   85

References and Notes 87

About the Author...93

In lieu of a foreword

Dear Professor E.O. Wilson

Thank you for your book *The Creation – An Appeal to Save Life on Earth*[1]. I have read it with great interest. And thank you for the gift of "biophilia" which translates into love of life. You discovered that love of life is innate to humans, and you were the first one to describe the phenomenon. The term philia is of course used in many words. For me one always stands out: Philadelphia. In the euphoria of the enlightenment the Americans named their First City "Brotherly Love". What a great concept! Not even the French, the fathers of the enlightenment went that far. Instead they inscribed fraternitè, or brotherhood, on their banners. However, as a term or concept 'Philadelphia' has much greater connotations. It doesn't just mean solidarity, but love. Obviously Philadelphia did not remain the capital of the nation, neither politically, spiritually or idealistically. What could have been a great opportunity to declare support and allegiance to such a noble concept was dead before it was born. Was the American dream in reality just the desire to become rich? Or had this dream originally contained a spiritual underpinning in "Brotherly Love", which would act as a regulator for our dealings not only with one another, but also with all of nature, its resources and even our economy? Whatever the answer might be, this chance was lost, and maybe because of that we find ourselves in such a dire situation as you describe it: that we are now facing the prospect of an unlivable planet by the end of this century due to the irreversible damage to the biosphere and subsequent loss of biodiversity. And you are certainly not alone in ringing the alarm bells. We hear the tolling all over the world and from different quarters. Thank you for the passion in which you inform us, and thank you for reaching out to other professions with your call to save life on earth. I certainly share your concern.

You address your book fictitiously to "Dear Pastor". Since I'm a pastor myself, I take your book as an invitation to join you in your mission and I gladly accept the opportunity. Of course you remember the pastor of your childhood and youth, who was a literalist and Southern Baptist. You no longer share this brand of faith. Neither do I. In fact I never have since I was raised and became a minister of the Lutheran Church in former East Germany. As you can imagine this was a tough climate to be a minister in, for militant atheism was the official state doctrine. I could not afford to have my head in the clouds, nor did I ever expect to be saved by a rapture in midair. I do not believe in the letter of the Bible, I believe in the God of the Bible. I encouraged my congregation to bring their brains with them to church.

"Do not park it with your car", I used to say jokingly, don't hang it up with your hat. We've got to love God with all our heart, with all our soul and all our mind, as the greatest commandment says. "Mind" of course I interpret as our ability to reason. I do believe that God so loved the world…that (we)…shall not perish (John 3: 16). Don't you agree that this is a pretty good safety railing to rely on while we hike together the treacherous trail of trying to save life on earth? Treacherous indeed and a formidable task. For what is wrong with us is not just a technical glitch which could be fixed, nor is it a moral failure. It is rather a lack of love and compassion of which 'biophilia' is a facet. As you observed, love is deeply engrained in us, and is innate. As a pastor I add: it's even the foundation of the world. But love within us is overgrown and constantly choked by other inherited traits, predominantly that of hunting and gathering, which I will explain at greater depth in chapter 4. This is a thought pattern of our ancestral past that we must tame in order to survive. We have to aim higher, and therefore we have to change.

This letter introduces my call to challenge our global society to aim for a higher civilization. I am appealing to world leaders in politics, science, and religion to help stabilize our situation. By looking at the world around me, I have come to believe that we are about to lose our balance. With all the weight of our technological and economical progress we can no longer stand on just *one* leg: the Charter of Human Rights and Freedoms. Although it is extremely important even in its undeveloped form, unfortunately even this rudimentary leg is not fully implemented. To find our balance we have to bring down a second leg, which I will call the Charter of Love and Compassion. In the chapters to come I will explain what that means and how I think it can be implemented.

However, before I can do this, we will have to look carefully for the root causes of our problems. The problems themselves, such as environmental degradation, pollution and climate change, loss of biodiversity, the constant economic problems we have, the military threats we face etc, are not my topic per se. I won't add any new charts or numbers nor will I advocate for the environment or social justice. These are important tasks and I'm grateful to the scientists and advocates who take them on. However, my task is different: I am asking how we came to face these difficulties, and what caused them in the first place. In order to accomplish this very difficult task, I will keep my nose to the ground and trod slowly and carefully even if it means taking a detour. I will not raise my head up into the air and pretentiously proclaim, "I smell human sin" and then quote chapter and verse from the Bible or another sacred book. Instead I'm looking for the root causes of our dilemma in history and evolution, as well as in our human makeup of inherited genetic or psychological traits. Only once we are able to formulate a diagnosis can we then begin to look for a cure. However, I will need help from real experts like you, Professor.

I greet you with "Philadelphia"
Yours truly,
Pastor Friedmut Wilhelm, dipl. theol. M.div.

world. There were our mothers and aunts, fathers and neighbors - people who did so much for us and didn't ask for pay or profit. I think of the countless volunteers, without whom our communities, schools, our hospitals, churches or cultural institutions would not run. These people are wonderful signs that new beginnings are possible. I think this way about every person. No matter how crusty and grumpy someone has become, for him too a new morning dawns. Even the hardened criminal – I see him as a baby in his mother's arms. He was clean, fresh, and innocent, and consequently hope and change are possible.

I see, how far we have come as a global community. It was only in 1948 that we received the Declaration of Human Rights. But already so many countries now have a charter of human rights and freedoms, enforceable before the courts. We have international conventions and protocols, and if some countries have not yet signed on or still claim exemption, I'm confident that for them a new day will come too.

I look at science and what scientists tell us about their work. The advancements are breathtaking. New enchanting worlds are opening up before our eyes, and we begin to recognize our place in the universe, with its vast distances, and the duration since the big bang. When we zoom in on our little planet earth and to the moment when the first person jumped out of the tree of life – "Adam" the Hebrews called him – we see how he stepped back and looked at where he had come from and felt so lonely: the universe looked at itself. This is the most astonishing thing, the greatest wonder: through our reflective mind the universe recognizes itself! I see modern technology in a positive light too. Not only the amenities that changed our lives so much since the days of our grandparents, but also the communication technology that has brought us closer together worldwide. I can see and talk to my grandchildren in Korea from my home in Canada, or see and talk to my friend in Peru. One day we might be able to decipher signals from outer civilizations and begin text messaging across the galaxy.

Globalization is to be celebrated. Hopefully it will allow us to eventually lose our xenophobia. In Canada we benefit from our cultural diversity. I see our society as a bouquet of flowers, native ones, exotic ones -, all colors contributing to the whole. It's a beautiful world.

The world is the paradise.

I often think of it as a symphony. It might start with a big bang, some percussions, a whirlwind of strings – there is the theme, only to get lost again. And now the various instruments try to find it. The harp feels around, a flute, the strings search again, more wood instruments contribute - till the theme slowly emerges. Now all the various sections of the orchestra lift it up and it rises in a triumphant crescendo. We in the audience are lifted up too and might feel the ceiling of the concert hall rises above us. And indeed, such music touches the ceiling of the universe and reaches for eternity. Then it ebbs away, playing with the theme graciously till the music comes to its glorious end.

In the evolution of the universe, we, the human race have reached the point where we are just about to hear the theme of creation. Individually we might just play a little fiddle, but together, collectively, we will recognize it, lift it up in celebration. Would it not be too bad to leave the hall now, to close the paradise for good, just because some old habits lead us astray? It's too good a life, too wonderful a world to lose it now.

CHAPTER 2

DEFINING MOMENTS

Professor, the summer of 2008 became a defining time for me, an ecological awakening or enlightenment, if you will, that changed my life. Not that I was ignorant in ecological matters before. As a public speaker I had to be informed, and good stewardship of the "resource" earth had always been an article of faith for Lutherans. However, there were two events that summer that changed the way I think. The first one I will forever remember with the image of

The MAN in the DARK SUIT

I spent all of June 2008 traveling in Germany. I had nothing in my appointment book except a Cultural Festival at Görlitz in East Germany at the end of the month where I had been asked to preach at an interfaith service. The three-day festival centered around integration of different cultures into the new Europe. However, when I landed in Frankfurt, several other topics dominated the news. Europe was abuzz with anxious discussions. Al Gore's explosive bestseller "An Inconvenient Truth" had just hit the bookstores. With graphs, pictures and rational analysis Gore put his emphasis on climate change and its potential catastrophic consequences. Several other publications by biologists like yourself, Professor, and historians appeared around the same time. They all pointed in the same direction and held the same ominous message: unless we change immediately and dramatically we could lose our place on a livable planet by the end of the century. And like in any good drama there was a Savior, a white knight who entered the scene. Barack Obama had just become the front-runner in the race for the American presidency and he preached hope and change. But an immediate challenge presented itself to his ambitions and promises when a financial crisis began to unfold, such as the world had not seen since the 1930s. Another bubble burst at the stock market and America was the instigator. They had supported their booming housing market by selling cheap mortgages to people who did not have enough income to qualify for them. These cheap mortgages were then packaged and labeled "excellent investment backed by real estate" and sold internationally. And the world bought it and so became accomplices to the instigators. Millions and millions lost their savings when the bubble burst. Bankers on the other hand collected fat bonuses. Charges were never laid. Take all this together and you have a perfect drama. All you need now is a venue to bring it to the stage. The venue came by accident: in June 2008

Germany was hosting the European Soccer Cup (or football championship as they call it). This meant there was a nationwide party going on. In private homes, in public squares, in front of huge screens, on sidewalks. As I walked by such scene, I heard someone say: "you want a beer, Sir, come, sit down". I stopped and looked, a middle-aged woman nodded at me: "yes, I'm serious, sit down, you are not from here, are you?" When I told her that I was from Canada everyone started talking at the same time, and there were quite a few people, families and friends from the neighborhood it seemed. Now they moved to the side so I could have a seat. Canada seemed to be the land of their dreams: green, endless, land of the Indians and Eskimos as they still call our Inuits. "Six months of winter" I added. "But what about the Arctic, is the sea ice melting? And how are the Polar Bears doing?" And with that we were in a nationwide discussion of environment related issues, which would go on day after day for the three weeks of my travels. Climate change topped the charts together with the wellbeing of the biosphere, followed by concerns over the economy. Everyone was discussing the question of human greed and "how much do we really need to be happy". Wherever I went it was the same party, with a beer in their hand and a screen to watch the game, these people seemed so content and in such celebratory mood and yet the anxious question was lingering: for how long can the party go on? Sure, the championship would be over by the end of the month. But the greater party, the party of 'life on earth' - could it last - ? Was there anything anyone could do to make it last ?

I was extremely glad that I had this opportunity; it felt like I had my hand at the pulse of a nation. I felt a tremor of angst but also a lot of good will.

One day I asked a grocer at a corner store what he thought of Obama, the new hopeful for the American presidency. Immediately we were surrounded by a dozen curious people. One remarked: "change yes, but Obama has to tell us what change. He has to be profoundly different."

I usually stayed with friends of mine. When I retired to their home in the evening, the party went on. I also stayed with a pastor friend who told me to stop worrying, "you are not the Savior. Your job is to preach the Good News, no matter what the circumstances are, and to comfort those who are in distress". But how can I restrain myself, how can I not worry? Are we not supposed to be guardians and caretakers of this beautiful earth? Are we not responsible to those who lived before us and those who come after us, our children and grandchildren. Those who shaped our world with their ideas, culture, art and philosophy and those who would inherit their dreams but also the reality of a world in deep trouble.

At one point I also stayed with a doctor. When I asked her if there is something wrong with our human brain, she laughed. "Look at it" I said "the cerebrum has taken over, we are ruled by the part of the brain where our reasoning is located. But the cerebellum, the part responsible for our instincts has been marginalized.

Consequently, our instincts are almost non-functional. Are there any mammals that are able to commit suicide or kill their own species? Their instincts prevent them from doing so. Not ours anymore, we kill ourselves and our own. Think of a suicide bomber who blows himself up and hundreds of others with him. He has no mechanism built in to prevent this from happening. Our whole way of life, our unfettered consumerism, our economy and our relentless pursuit of happiness and fortune are like one giant suicide bomb that can wipe us and other life forms off the face of the earth." The doctor had not answered my question of an imbalanced brain. And that was alright, since questions are often more important than answers. They put us on our way while answers stop us. To be on the way is what life is all about.

Three weeks of discussions on many different levels; three weeks of beer and soccer. When my time was over and the event at Görlitz had passed, I was totally exhausted mentally and physically. I could only form one thought: "let's get out of here, let's get home to the solitude of our acreage in Northern Alberta". I could not stay one more night in Berlin, so instead I decided to rent a hotel room in Frankfurt and sleep a good twelve hours before departure. That night in Frankfurt, when I thought I had made up my mind and would leave these crazy weeks behind me, I met the man in the dark suit.

I had been driving all day from Berlin to Frankfurt. I returned my car at the airport and was immediately shuttled to a small hotel not too far away in a quiet semi-industrial neighborhood. I saw a sign of Lufthansa but had really no idea where I was. In my exhaustion I barely registered the hotel room I was assigned. Fortunately, anything with a bed would have been sufficient. However, despite my overwhelming need to sleep, it was suppertime and I was very hungry. Thus I strolled out into the warm evening to find a place to eat. Unlike the constant parties and activities I had seen since I had arrived, the streets here were empty. Warehouses, and industrial yards echoed with the unfamiliar silence. I could make out some apartments further west but no shops or restaurants close by. Finally I saw a man in a dark suit approaching a crosswalk, and I asked him for directions. He was not from here, he said, but knew that there was a Turkish bistro nearby. It took me some time to find the place, but when I did I was pleased to see a lovely stone terrace, garden furniture, and elegant umbrellas providing shade from the warm sun. However, every table seemed to be occupied. Fortunately, at a table in the far corner sat the man in the dark suit. He nodded at me and pointed at a chair beside him. Hot, tired, and feeling lost in this unfamiliar surrounding I gladly accepted. A quick glance told me that the man was probably in his late forties, he was clean-shaven, with an athletic figure and intelligent blue eyes. He raised the beer that he had just been served and nodded warmly at me.

Something about him made me feel safe to blurt out, "I'm here only for one night, tomorrow I'm going back home to Canada, thank God!"

"I have to stay a little longer", the man said, "I'm from Austria".

"Ooh", I stretched, "I'm so happy, no more soccer parties, no more beer".

However, as those words left my mouth, all of my mental excitement and discussion of the past four weeks returned to me. Almost unaware of myself and without intention I asked

"What do you think about climate change?"

"Climate change? It's real, it's happening", he said, looking at his watch. "The consequences will be catastrophic, but there is nothing that can be done anymore. Too late."

And just like that he began to eat.

"Too late?" I said, "I fear that you are right. Things will run their course. But should we not take certain measures to be prepared for a new start?"

"What measures?" he asked between mouthfuls.

"The problem" I replied, "is man. Man lost his orientation, and therefore also lost his roots. We are like drift wood in the vast ocean of the universe. Nobody seems to know where we are or where we came from. And that is why nobody cares what is happening. We need to show people our place in the universe. That's a prerequisite for change."

I was now being served while the man in the dark suit had pushed his plate aside. He stared far beyond me, as if he saw something, slowly he wiped his lips and fingers, then folded his napkin and abruptly stood up.

"Sir, I have to go, a meeting to attend. Thank you for the conversation. I did not expect that tonight. You are absolutely right that orientation is the key. I leave you with one question though. Where are we going? You have to answer this too or there won't be real orientation. I don't ask you for a new utopia. I ask the age-old question, which is a transcendental one: where are we going? The meaning of it all. Das 'Wohin', mein Herr, das 'Wohin'" (these were the only German words he said, "The where, Sir the where') He bowed politely towards me and left.

The question 'wohin' has never left me since. Where are we going?

The other event of defining quality was much closer to home and outright scary. I call it: the making of Armageddon

*Our daughter Thekla
with James and their children*

The MAKING of ARMAGEDDON

Our daughter is a science teacher who teaches Math and Physics in Senior High. I remember you, Professor, saying that Math is just a language, but the learning of this language is hampered by math phobia, "the curse of homo sapiens in training".[2] Thekla is a very creative math teacher, I believe, who in part writes her own textbooks with a lot of funny features and good humor. She is highly in demand as a teacher at international schools abroad. Working with her husband, they move with their three children to various schools around the world. That summer they had finished one contract in the Middle East and were now on their way to their next job in another part of the world with a stopover in Edmonton, Alberta. We were delighted to have them with us for a few days, catching up on what had happened since we saw them last and getting to know our grandchildren a little better. Together we were cruising down the freeway that afternoon towards Edmonton where our son had invited us for a barbecue and family reunion, when Thekla started a conversation with the kids obviously trying to find out how the curriculum for math in Canada compared to that at the international schools. The conversation turned quickly into a math exam. I say quickly for Thekla talked so fast and gave so little time for the kids to answer that it seemed as if she was reading out loud from a sheet of paper. When the kids gave up by throwing their hands into the air, Thekla accelerated even more, now blurting the answers out herself – problem-solution, problem-solution till she was exhausted herself. "I can't continue anymore", she said with a toneless voice. She had fallen back into her seat, her face pale and her lips quivering. 'What jetlag can do to people' I thought, 'or was it the change from a desert climate to that of Northern Canada, or just the stress of moving again.' I didn't worry about this bizarre behavior. Sure, we would have a good get-together, it was such a beautiful afternoon, and I didn't want to worry. Once more Thekla talked while we were driving, how she had been honored as the best teacher of the Province in her first year. "They offered me an Oxford scholarship" she said, "but my family comes first", and then she gave a whole list of other achievements and again rattled them off as if she was reading out loud from a book. We had never heard anything of that nor do we do such boasting in our family, and Thekla never had. But thank God, we had now arrived at our destination and we would have a good time, eager to forget what had just happened. And so it seemed: a great welcome and hello right in the backyard. The children running around, the adults embracing each other, the dog barking and jumping with excitement till things settled down and those in charge got busy with the food and drinks. My wife and I had stepped further into the yard followed by Thekla. It is one of those places where anything green is allowed to grow. You would have loved it, Professor: biodiversity in the centre of the city. Nothing is manicured, no herbicides, no pesticides, no chemical fertilizers and no traps for slugs, let it grow, let it crawl, a self regulated biotope.

And yet they manage to have a sizable vegetable patch and grow usable plants of all sorts. Thekla looked with amazement at all the produce, ready to be harvested. She hadn't seen that in the Arabic desert, where she had spent the last two years. I of course knew that we had a drought for several years now ourselves and that regions of the province had turned desert like. Across the province ranchers couldn't find feed for their cattle and trees were dying everywhere. In comparison, this backyard was an oasis. All of this might have reminded me of my discussions in Germany and offhandedly I asked Thekla what she thought of climate change. She threw me a quick glance and quipped:

"Climate change is real, nothing we can do. It's too late. Let's not talk about it, dad, come."

And with that she took my arm and we went back to the deck. She sat down. Others were still coming and going. My wife and I sat down too. Suddenly Thekla straightened herself and moved forward to the edge of her seat. Now I could see her face, her lips quivering. In the car I had only the occasional glance in the rear mirror. But now I saw her eyes, unable to focus as she began reading out loud from yet another page.

"There is no future for our children, Dad. The waters are rising, where will people go? The polar caps melting. The river deltas will be flooded, salty marshes, what were once the bread baskets for millions and millions. Where will the people of Bangladesh go? And the people from India and China? The Himalayan glaciers melting, their big rivers Ganges, Brahmaputra, Yellow River, Jangtsekiang, they all dry up. Billions of people will be on the move into Siberia, Russia, Australia. There will be terrible slaughter, war as never seen before, survival of the meanest and quickest. But not for long. Diseases will take the rest, with all the human biomass and the unsanitary conditions. You can't escape. Not even in Canada. Your American cousins will come up here, now skeletons themselves, and drink from the last puddles on the Canadian Shield. Thekla's voice had risen in pitch and volume as she spoke, and was now close to screaming. Suddenly she fell almost silent and mumbled to herself: "But the children, the children…"

I was shocked both by the rationality of her speech as by the way she seemed to be suffering through it. When she got up I saw beads of sweat on her forehead. I tried to take her into my arms and tell her not to count God out of her hopes. But she did not hear me. Instead she drew her arms away from me and walked towards the house. As she entered, the last of the family arrived, and the food was brought out. Everyone began to eat, and it was not until some were filling up for a second time when Thekla's husband noticed that his wife wasn't there.

James went in. When he finally came back he seemed extremely disturbed. With a low voice and very slowly – like somebody who tries to keep his emotions under control – he said:

"Thekla is in trouble. She is locked in the bathroom. At first I could talk to her and she made some sounds. But then she fell silent all together. Somebody help me to get the door open."

Now everyone was rushing about. The men hurried

in to open the door. The children put their hands before their open mouths and made helpless gestures to each other. My head was spinning. What could this be? Did she not have a brain surge twice, once in the car, then here? A brain surge is sometimes reported to happen just before an epileptic seizure. I was gripped with worry. Could it be a stroke or even a brain tumor? O my God, our daughter! We must rush her to the hospital!

When they brought her out, she seemed to be wrapped in total apathy and consumed by utter weakness. Her face was pale and her features had dropped almost beyond recognition. Her hair was hanging in strands as if she had tried to pull it out. She seemed not to recognize anyone as they led her to the car and drove off quickly. The rest of us had to cope with our emotions, each in his own way. My wife and I were kind of lucky, for we had the children to distract us. We tried our best to shelter them from greater harm, but no matter what we adults are thinking, it is always the kids who shelter us with their worry–free and innocent outlook on life. I don't know how many hours we had spent with them, but we had just tucked them in for the night when the phone call came from the hospital. As soon as I could hear James' voice, I could see the bright smile on his face:

"We are all very happy here. Everything is alright. We are just back from a conference with the doctors. They didn't leave a stone unturned but found nothing - no stroke, no tumor. Rather, they agreed that it was a rare form of migraine when a patient seems to be left tangling between consciousness and unconsciousness.

Thekla is fine, we are so happy! What a bummer the whole thing."

After she came home that night and during the weeks she stayed with us, Thekla had no recollection of how she had gotten to the city nor what had happened at the garden patch or on the deck. However, I will never forget how terrified and concerned we were that night and then the big relief we experienced. It was an enormous and shocking experience. A shock when we plunged into our worst fears about Thekla's health; and when we came out of these fears, the big relief. But once we recovered from worrying about her health, our relief was overshadowed by another shock, about what she had actually said in the rattling manner as if she was reading out loud. Where did all this come from? First the perfect math exam, then the rational and coherent speech of apocalyptic dimensions! It seems impossible to me that her brain, under the onslaught of a severe migraine could have produced either of these performances at that moment. These things must have been in her, ready to come out. We all have a subconscious, where unneeded and unwanted things are stored and suppressed. There is a trap door to the subconscious that allows thoughts to escape only when we are unconscious, asleep, or under anesthetics. Then the door is more or less open and stuff can come up again, hence our dreams and nightmares. The migraine in Thekla's case - in ways unknown to me – unlocked the trap door to the subconscious and the thoughts stored there were able to come out. With the perfect math exam it is easy to explain. She had done many of those exams with her classes. And by marking them she had reread them dozens of times. Once the test results were announced these exams were not needed anymore. They would only clutter the teacher's brain and that's why they were allowed to float down to the basement of the subconscious, to return only when the trap door was open. With Thekla's other speech, her apocalyptic forecast, it's a different matter. She most likely never sat down to design such presentation. It's rather that snippets of information had reached her through the media, through journals and magazines. The same way that all of us ingest tiny pieces of information without realizing or noting it. More or less we are all informed that climate change is here and that the results can be catastrophic. These snippets of information are very disturbing and worrisome. Before they can develop into a nightmare of apocalyptic proportions we send them down to the basement, to our subconscious, "Let's not talk about it" – and we forget.

What I learned from our daughter's incident is that we know, but prefer not to know. The knowledge of an impending catastrophe is in all of us but it is stored deep down in our subconscious. However, if it comes to the surface it can be very comprehensive knowledge, as Thekla demonstrated. She tells a story with a beginning and an end: climate change and rising sea levels, loss of arable land around rivers, estuaries, and deltas. There are geographical coordinates: Bangladesh, India, China. She names mountains and rivers that are drying up. Huge populations are forced to move, wars are ensuing and pandemics break out. However, not everything that ails us was included. She didn't mention the loss of biodiversity, which concerns you so much, Professor. To fill in this gap, let me give a little report on what I have learned from you.

The earth's biodiversity is threatened. Biodiversity is the multiplicity of all forms of life on earth that make up the biosphere. Any loss of species narrows the diversity of the biosphere.

I personally think of it this way: the earth has a very thin and delicate skin. This virtual skin is the biosphere - life in all its forms, whether in water or on land. The health of this biosphere depends on biodiversity. It is all one skin: big animals and small ones, big trees and small plants, microbes and insects so numerous that it defies imagination. All these make up the layers and cells of the skin. I say "layers and cells of the skin" because the biosphere is not simply the sum of all living things, but rather one interrelated and interdependent system or living organism that spans the earth like a filigree veil. The loss of species, a loss of biodiversity, rips holes into the veil. Every species depends on another one as food source, as host or shelter, and as healer and promoters. Humans ought to be keepers and guardians of this biosphere, rather than relentless invaders who take away the living space of others. We don't even know how much we have already lost. Just think of the vast areas we have under cultivation for food production. We have taken these areas away from other species, fenced them in and made them sterile through the use of pesticides and herbicides. These areas are so big, that they can be seen from outer space like spots and blemishes on the skin of Mother Earth. We know how doctors carefully examine spots and blemishes on our human skin to make sure they are not cancerous. Biologists are the researchers and doctors of the skin of Mother Earth, of the biosphere. They ring the alarm bells and call on us: "please, help us to save life on earth".

Conclusion

We have surveyed the landscape. We have heard from Thekla, deep out of her subconscious what climate change can do, that there might be no future for our children, when the waters rise and wars ensue and diseases spread relentlessly. We have learned that the delicate skin of Mother Earth is at risk, the biosphere that is depleted by human activity.

Any of these challenges or a combination of some or all of them can lead to a catastrophic meltdown of global dimension. This critical point will most likely be reached towards the end of this century, when the population has peaked and demographically aged. Similar catastrophes of this magnitude have happened in the past. They happened five times during the last 400 million years. The last one happened 65 million years ago, when most of the land animals, including the dinosaurs, died.

It was a cosmic catastrophe then, when a giant meteorite hit the Mexican Yucatan Peninsula shaking the crust of the earth so, that volcanic eruptions occurred around the world. The amount of ashes and dust in the air caused a global winter, which led to mass extinctions of plants and animals on land and at sea. After each of these five catastrophies, it took mother nature 5 to 10 million years to repair the damage to her delicate skin. This time, after the only man made catastrophe, it would take an equal amount of time. This is not an option for human beings who have only an individual lifespan of less than a hundred years. We have to act now and act decisively.

How come, one might ask, if the situation is so grim, why for heavens sake is nobody talking, why so little from the media, why was this not a topic in recent elections, why is nobody screaming? Our daughter Thekla gave the answer "let's not talk about it, Dad". Why not? Because she could not live with this knowledge. It would have driven her out of her mind. So she shoved it down into the subconscious – not willingly, but instinctively.

We, as a society and civilization have a collective subconscious. If things become too burdensome or too frightening we put a spin on those stories and try to forget them. We couldn't live with the knowledge that we have only a window of a few decades to turn things around or else face the collapse of our world. So we suppress the information and begin to live in total denial. Let's not point fingers and blame each other or raise suspicions of a conspiracy. If there is one, we are all part of it. It's normal human nature to do so since it's our way to survive the present day. However, I'm deeply grateful to all the scientists, politicians and people of knowledge, who look beyond the present day and want us to survive those crucial decades, and to have a future for our children. 'Wake up, man', they seem to say, 'you are sleeping behind the wheel. Hit the brakes or you will drive off the bridge'. But we tend to doze off again. 'It's not going to happen'. 'Man always adapts', 'these things come in cycles'. And we go off to sleep.

Before you do and I lose you, I invite you on a trip to meet our grandmother. I invite you to fly with us to Ethiopia to meet Lucy. Just remember as you pack your bags for the trip: we are now searching for the root cause of humanity's troubles.

*My wife Gundula visiting with Lucy
in Addis Abeba*

CHAPTER 3

LUCY

We spent Christmas 2006 in Dubai. Our sons had decided to visit their sister and her family, so they could be together at a time when most families meet. Godparents to some of the kids, they brought their presents. My wife and I then followed. Why sit at home alone? But since we both had been to Dubai the year before and done all the sightseeing and more, we wanted to add something to the trip and booked a flight to Addis Abeba, Ethiopia. There we knew Christmas to be 12 days later and we would be able to celebrate a second time. Ethiopia has some of the world's most ancient traditions. Not only is their church one of the oldest, probably going back directly to the disciple Philip, Ethiopia is also as far as I know the only country in the world, that at least in part had converted to the faith of Abraham, which later became known as the Jewish faith. It goes back to around 1000 BC, when Queen Sheba paid a royal visit to Jerusalem, where King Salomon resided. She found the King impressive in his wisdom and splendor. Among the gifts she brought, were a hundred and twenty talents of gold and an enormous quantity of spices. In return Salomon gave the Queen "all she desired, whatever she asked". (1 King 10: 13) Among those gifts was a son. We learned about this gift, and the resulting diplomatic situation while we were in Ethiopia. Subsequently, all the kings of Ethiopia claimed to be descendants of King Salomon. One of them, Lalibela, who lived in the twelfth century AD ordered the building of eleven churches in a short period of time in a small village, called after the King Lalibela. We heard that they were built by the hands of men and of angels. The men worked during the day, the angels at night. This was justified because otherwise it could never have been accomplished in such a short period of time, especially when there were no contemporary buildings of note. Instead, that time period produced only round mud huts with thatched roofs. Even the King did not have a proper house but rather lived in a cave-like room beside the entrance of one of the churches. The marvel doesn't end there. These churches were not built by masons who set stone upon stone. They were created by sculptors, who carved them out of rock. They resemble Byzantine Romanic architecture with their narrow windows, vaulted ceilings, columns and capitals, nave and narthex. We would have made the trip simply to see that. And we were richly rewarded, especially by the sight of tens of thousands of pilgrims in their white cotton tunics, the women with their headscarves, some of the men sporting huge umbrellas as they descended on the village from the surrounding hills. And yet, in spite of all the ancient marvels and the most picturesque Christmas celebration we had ever seen, it all paled in comparison to what we were to see in Addis Abeba: Lucy, our grandmother.

Lucy resides on the ground level of the National Museum in Addis Abeba. She is a petit lady of a stunning beauty and startling nakedness. She is bone-naked and one million years old, the oldest human being ever found. Her skeleton was recovered from the highlands of Ethiopia in the 20th century. Her age makes her the Grand Mother of us all. And this makes all Ethiopians proud. Man's cradle stood in Africa, in these mountains, not too far from the source of the Blue Nile. I had hoped to kiss her hand or – if protocol would allow – give her a fleeting embrace. But no, she was behind glass. Like the pope, when he tours the world. How can you communicate through bulletproof glass and over a distance of a million years? I stepped back a little and looked at her. At first she offered me nothing - no smile from a skull. But as I looked through her frame focusing on a point behind her, I saw her face taking shape. Her lips began to cover her mouth, full lips. Yes, I saw her face blush, could see the rose color shining through her dark skin, saw her sparkling eyes and how she quickly raised her hand to shelter them from the light, which she hadn't seen for a million years. I looked at her rib cage and counted 12 ribs on each side, a slender breastbone, and strong backbone. In that cage I envisioned her heart beating in expectation while it was young, slowing in resignation when she grew older. And yet a heart so big that everyone had a place in it, her parents, her mate, her children. Was it a heart of love and compassion? I saw her hand again as she was steadying her toddler, teaching him to walk upright and free. I saw her hand waving to her mate, luring him to the back of the cave. The same hand, now behind glass, caressing his chest and groin, as the two engaged to become one.

The last bone I dared to study was her pelvis. I know it is not decent to stare so closely at a lady's most private parts. But this shall be said: Lucy's pelvis is the gate through which we all passed. This is your Arc de Triomphe Lucy! We salute you and will hold you in our heart forever, Grand Mother that you are.

––––––––––––––––––––

A million years ago, when Lucy was still at her cave, one morning her sons came to her and said:

"Mom, we are going to leave."

"Alright" she said, "go, hurry. I want to know what to prepare for dinner tonight."

"Oh mom, you don't understand, we are not coming back."

"So", Lucy said, "you are afraid you might not come back? Then stay home. Are there predators around stalking you? Don't go, we'll survive a day or two."

"Oh mom, you really don't get it", the sons said. "We are going to an other land, land that has much game to hunt and trees to gather fruit from. Take care, mom!"

Lucy came out of her cave and quickly raised her hand to shelter her eyes from the sun. She saw them go across the plain. The boys ahead, the girls following. Hunters and gatherers for a million years. She felt her heart slowing in resignation. She went inside to the back of the cave and lay down, her face against the wall. That's how they found her – a million years later.

————————————

Lucy's children hiked from the Ethiopian plateau south into the savanna of what is now Kenya. They never forgot where they had come from. The mountains, where their mother's grave was, became an idealized memory, the land of brave adventures and real men. But they loved the unobstructed view of the African savanna, the big solitary trees and little bushes. They knew that animals would seek shelter there from the heat of the day. They loved the waterfront of lakes and rivers, where the animals came at dusk providing easy game.

A cottage at the waterfront, with great mountains behind us, monumental trees and "a view" over meadows and hills. Does this scene sound familiar? Scientists tell us that our preference of habitat, and the surroundings of our dream home is encoded in our genes from the time when our ancestors, the children of Lucy, lived on the African savanna. [3]

Eventually these people spread out and moved north, over long periods of time. First seasonally, then permanently they crossed the fertile crescent, which is now the Middle East, into Asia and Europe. There, in Europe, they met another human race, their distant cousins, the Neanderthals. Their reaction was horror, xenophobia. Had they never met another race? Or had they always just reacted in the same way?

The Neanderthals had larger brains than we have. They were gentle cave dwellers, who produced some fine fresco art. But, more importantly, they must have had a sense of compassion, for they cared for their sick, sometimes for many years.[4]

When the children of Lucy, who were now called Cro Magnons, saw the Neanderthals, they killed them. If they met other cousins or races (for instance in Asia) they killed them too. They appear to have been compulsive genocidal. By 15,000 years ago the Cro Magnons had established themselves as the only ones who the world would call one day homo sapiens. They had fought a war over 30,000 years, a war of killing, expulsion and absorption. The Neanderthals had then disappeared and with them their health care system. It would take another 15,000 years before something similar would appear but not cost-free as the Neanderthal's was.

How was it that Lucy's children became genocidal? Was it because they mercilessly left their mother behind?

How come that mankind, with all his aspirations and distinguished achievements in science, fine arts, philosophy, and religion still goes to war to kill other humans and that no one receives more medals and honors than those who return (or not) from the slaughter of the battlefields?

The traits we have inherited were encoded into our brains over a period of a million years. Old habits die hard. It has been a mere ten thousand years since Lucy's children changed their ways, began to grow their food and domesticate animals and eventually established the first civilization. This is too short a period for evolution to wash out the old traits and encode new ones.

While the two traits, which I mentioned, the choice of habitat and the genocidal trait are well described by researchers and we have begun to deal with them, we hear very little and do nothing about our most prevalent inheritance from the stone age: the habitual hunting and gathering. For millions of years a useful and necessary way of life, hunting and gathering is still written all over the face of our modern society. It is written permanently into our soul as if set into stone. It has taken on a life of its own, has become a law unto itself and is the single most important cause for the world's immanent destruction. It deserves its own chapter. I call it:

Hunters and Gatherers Unlimited

CHAPTER 4

HUNTERS and GATHERERS UNLIMITED

Man is a creature of habit. He does, what he is programmed to do. In this he is not different from animals. However, man can rationalize his habits, and can distinguish the good ones from the bad ones. He can throw out old habits that are obsolete and adopt new ones that promise a future. Everyone can do this individually for himself through rational thought process and by consciously forming the will to change. We also can do it collectively through education and culture. However, it will be a lifelong process, and any real collective change will begin with changing ourselves individually. While this appears to be a formidable task, anything less will be just stopgap measures, which will fail in the long run. However, for the moment they might buy us the time we need to widen our window of change.

The habit of hunting and gathering was acquired and deeply engrained into our fabric over a period of millions of years.[5)] Each morning it was the same thing: get up, go out, hunt and gather, come home with what you found and be rewarded. The reward being a warm meal at night and sometimes a pat on the shoulder: you are a good hunter like your dad or as Nimrod[6] was.

The reward for a good hunter could be status and prestige. As a result, his chances to get the most desirable mate would increase. Each day the same: get up, go out, hunt and gather, come home and be rewarded. Each day for Lucy's children was the same for millions of years. It worked for them for that long as a sustainable lifestyle. Not that these people got in any way rich, for they most likely barely scraped by. After all, life was very dangerous for them. By walking upright, man had taken a risk. The exposure of his soft belly and his throat, combined with the lack of claws or carnivorous teeth, made him more vulnerable, and the fact that he was not the best runner or climber forced him to rely on his senses of sight and hearing and his excellent memory. Of course, unlike other animals he could also rely upon the advantage of his fists. With his fists he could swing a bat in defense or to kill. He could throw a stone and kill a rabbit. However, in the way of self-defense he didn't have many options. Men were hunters, women and children more likely the gatherers. And yet, they were even more vulnerable. They mostly gathered under trees and in copses, searching for fire wood, roots and perhaps fruit to eat. A child was easily snatched by a predator, but so were women, even men did not always return. It was a dangerous world out there. The only safe place was around the fire. Due to the inherent danger of their lifestyle, and because both hunters and gatherers often returned empty-handed, the rule was adopted: 'take as much as you can'. It might give you an extra day or two in the safe zone of the fire side – time for leisure or time to think of something better than throwing rocks at rabbits.

We then have to adjust our formula for Stone Age living. It now reads:

'Get up, go out, hunt and gather, *take as much as you can,* come home and   be rewarded.'

This is the whole catechism of hunters and gatherers. It was the formula that was successfully followed day after day for millions of years and at the end of each day there was a reward. Every parent and every educator knows that repetition and reward works. "Constant dripping wears away the stone." The lesson is as timeless as the Colorado River grinding away at the red rocks of northern Arizona season after season for millions of years till the Grand Canyon was created. So the formula of stone age living - the catechism of hunters and gatherers - has edged itself into the human psyche and nothing would ever be able to get it out again. It sits so deep in us that it still encompasses our daily schedules, action plans and motivations to this day.

Lucy's children did quite all right for those millions of years. However, towards the end of the Paleolithic era, some 15,000 to 20,000 years ago, the equilibrium of powers was disturbed. Around the same time that they caused the complete extinction of the Neanderthals, the Cro Magnon also improved the arsenal of their weapons. With the invention of the spear they were able to keep a safe distance between themselves and their prey, consequently making them more successful in their hunting. With more food from their improved hunts, they could sustain more people, and thus the population began to grow. The kitchen scraps were eaten by dogs, which had followed man for quite a while, and eventually became domesticated. With new and improved technology, increased population, and eventually the help of dogs, the Cro Magnons were able to start hunting in grand style. They were then able to round up big game, spearing them en mass or driving them over steep cliffs. A senseless mass-slaughter began. 100,000 horses in one pile at Soultre in France, 1000 mammoth at Piedmost in Czech Republic.[7] We have to understand that this was an absolutely senseless slaughter. These hunters could not stockpile, preserve or consume 100,000 horses. They might have been able to live for a few days on horsemeat, but then the meat would rot. Why they nonetheless killed so much is encoded within Cro-Magnons psyche, the commandment etched in for millions of years: "take as much as you can and you will be rewarded". They simply could not stop "taking". For millions of years there was so little to take, but now with new weaponry they could take so much more, and so they compulsively did. The rewards were big not only for the top hunters who organized the party but also those who bravely and tirelessly brought down the most animals. They had the bragging rights, and their memory was kept alive around the campfires for centuries. We do not have to assume a 'darker side' of Lucy's children. They simply followed the rules, which were etched into their psyche. However, the consequences were catastrophic. During that period big game disappeared from all five inhabitable continents where the Cro Magnons/homo sapiens had spread. With their relentless killing and compulsive taking they had killed off their food base[8], which meant the end of hunting as they knew it. From 15,000 years ago the lifestyle of the Cro Magnons declined. During the Upper Paleolitic within a few thousand years we find fewer and fewer cave paintings till they stopped altogether. The tools they built became smaller and smaller. Only those adapting to smart gathering survived, mostly at lakeshores, in bogs and estuaries. The first stilt houses appear for instance at the shores of Lake Constance, Southern Germany.

During the Mesolithic period[9] people tried to survive on anything, including fish, roots, even grasses. It would take several thousand years more before man would learn to cultivate grasses, so this period was a time of great scarcity. It wasn't until the Neolitic era of 7,000 to 6,000 BC that agriculture emerged. People began to domesticate goats and sheep, to cultivate crops, and to live in communities, villages, and towns. Civilizations began to grow and prosper, but of course only in direct proportion to their food production. Just as the Cro Magnons over hunted their food supply, the Neolithic period saw the extension of production around the settlements until it was completely overextended. Transport lines became too long, and water became scarce the further one was from the river. Eventually, all trees had been cut for lumber, causing mass deforestation and the subsequent loss of arable land. Soil erosion came soon after, causing the collapse of the agricultural society. There are other classic examples of societies that destroyed their own environments through over productions. The Mayas in Central America and the people from Easter Island are two of the most notorious[10]. Like Lucy's children, they exploited their environment to the extent that they destroyed their food base. The Romans followed a similar pattern, although they lasted longer simply because they had an engineering mind and built roads and water ducts to transport food and water across great distances. They also enjoyed the advantage that their empire surrounded the Mediterranean Sea, providing waterways as the cheapest mode of transport to bring goods from far flung settlements. However, as the old forests were eventually all cut down in Italy and the agricultural land became exhausted and could no longer sustain the one million population of Greater Rome, they abandoned the land and simply moved their food production into Spain. When Spain suffered the same fate as Italy and her soil eroded, they moved into North Africa, which was still well forested at that time and now became the breadbasket for Rome. The party in Rome known as 'bread and circuses' for a million people could go on for another two hundred years before Rome finally fell to the Vandals in 455 AD. Their defeat was largely due to the fact that the land around the Mediterranean basin was exhausted, and the empire was in general decline, particularly in the West. We can see the scars the Roman empire left behind today. Italy, Greece, the Middle East, North Africa and Spain all still suffer from deforestation and subsequent soil erosion. Rome had taken too much. It had done the same as the Cro Magnons, and destroyed its own food base. We know already why: 'take as much as you can, and enjoy your reward' – this deeply encoded rule had made them compulsive 'takers'.

Rather than following this pattern through its various incarnations through the Middle Ages, I will leap forward to the Industrial Revolution and our own day and age. I can do this because nothing has really changed with man in an evolutionary sense. We are still the same as the Cro Magnons, having the same brain, hands, eyes, and ears. We have not evolved in the last 30,000 years, at least not noticeably. If we were able to snatch a child from that long ago and put it through our Kindergarten, school, and college this child would most likely do as well as our own children and maybe better. Rather than evolving, we have simply developed better tools to extend our reach, just as the Cro Magnon did. The industrial revolution of the eighteenth century with its enormous scientific advances, the mechanization of human production and the use of fossil fuel eventually enabled us to make machines that produce tools, those tools allow us to make better machine tools. There seems to be no limit how we can extend our reach - the reach of our eyes with the help of microscopes and telescopes; the reach of our ears with phones that allow us to hear through the airwaves; the reach of our hands so far, that we can do delicate surgeries over distances of thousands of miles.

And with our extended reach we can take more. We proudly call ourselves a consumer society; a society of takers. And like our hunting and gathering ancestors the Cro Magnons, we ignore our limits and become compulsive takers. Despite all warnings that there are 'limits to growth' [11)], we insist on an economic model based on constant expansion. We have come to believe in progress in an almost religious manner, which caters to our innate urge to take. We are genetically Hunters and Gatherers Unlimited, and we seem to be proud of it. This is the diagnosis for the ailment, which harms us the most and threatens to kill us at this time in our history. The venue for our hunting and gathering has changed. No longer the African Savanna but the factory floor, the office tower, and laboratory, and increasingly the banks and stock markets. That's where we are taking way too much, to the extent that we are destroying our own base. It is our own doing and happens essentially in three ways: through depletion, pollution, and encroachment of the environment.

Through depletion: any container has a limited content, which you can measure in liters, in tons, or megatons, but it is limited. The planet earth is such a container, so big – I admit – that I am unable to give the units in which to measure it. But it is still a container with a limited content. Some of the content nears depletion like fossils which we burn as fuel, or fertile land which is lost to desertification and rising sea levels, and certain species which we over hunt or over fish.

Through pollution: pollution is a dirty word, but pollutants are not necessarily dirty. They are chemicals that are found everywhere, even in our own bodies. Life evolved in a chemical environment. It uses a lot of chemicals as building blocks and tolerates others in concentrations it got used to. Through our industrial pollution, our warfare and consumption we disturb the equilibrium of the chemical environment through the discharge of chemicals in ever increasing concentration. While much has been written and said about the discharge of greenhouse gases into the atmosphere and the resulting global warming and while the standoff between climate change deniers and climate change witnesses continues, I want to draw your attention to our discharge of chemicals into the ocean. Everything we discharge either into the soil, rivers or the atmosphere is eventually washed into the sea. This has always been the way: the elements we find in the ground or in the air are also found in the waters of the oceans in certain concentrations, which makes the oceans the soup in which life can thriv. However, too much of a good thing can turn toxic. Balance is everything, and that's where the challenge arises. Through our human production we discharge an ever increasing amount of acidic substances, which eventually lead to an increased acidification of the oceans, particularly through the dissolving of carbon dioxide into the sea. This added acidity threatens the greatest life structures on earth, the coral reefs[12]. The reefs' coral polyps live in a very delicate symbiosis with a certain strain of algae called zooxanthellae, which grow on the polyps' surface. In return for the corals' hospitality the zooxanthellae feed their host through their ability to photosynthesize. Through added acidity of the ocean, and helped by rising water temperatures, the algae become toxic to the coral polyps and as a result are being expelled –

coral bleaching begins: the once colorful corals turn bony white and die. They would die for sure if they kept the toxic algae, and they die eventually if they expel them. I saw the coral bleaching myself recently at the Andaman Sea, where I marveled together with my family at the abundant life around the reefs. What I didn't know at the time was, that a quarter of all marine life depends on the coral reefs for habitat and shelter. Twenty five percent of all marine life, plants and animal alike, will loose their habitat and become the homeless of the world's oceans. Just imagine for a moment that a quarter of the human population, one and a half billion people would become homeless within a generation or two. The result would be a total breakdown of the global society as all our safety nets would fail, policing, health care, the economy etc. There is much more life in the oceans than on land. Therefore the numbers of the homeless would be much higher and the breakdown of the biological equilibrium in the oceans would be much more severe. Considering what we have learned, that the biosphere is mother earth's delicate skin where all cells are interrelated and interdependent including us, the catastrophe of the oceans would be the catastrophe of mankind. The oceans are not only one of the most important food resources for us; they also contain the largest gene pool, which becomes increasingly important for research and medicine.

Through encroachment

Finally our vastly extended reach *encroaches* on the living space of all other creatures. Did not our mothers teach us not to disturb a bird's nest? Through our extended reach we disturb virtually every creature's nest. 'Footprint' we call it, footprints from six billion people, and by the middle of the century three billion more. We expand and squeeze out other life forms as if the earth belongs only to us. 'You can not stop progress' we say, and with this progress we mean more human progress, but we do so at the expense of other life forms, not considering that their wellbeing is our wellbeing, for we are part of one organism called the biosphere.

————————————

In the above analysis I have summarized our ailments again and I have given the diagnosis. We are genetically Hunters and Gatherers Unlimited. Everyone can test this diagnosis while lying on his back at night, contemplating the day that has gone by and going through the plans and hopes for the coming day. Some people do this in their evening prayer. If you don't say such prayer, I suggest that you take the formula for Stone Age living, which I called the catechism of hunters and gatherers. Say it in your mind and see how it fits you. If it fits you well and makes you fall asleep peacefully, then you know that you are of the same makeup as Lucy's children, who went out to hunt and gather for a million years.

The Thinker, sculpture by Auguste Rodin.

CHAPTER 5

THE WEIRDNESS OF MAN and his GOODNESS

Or the genocidal/suicidal strain and bridge building

Professor, we have hiked a long way now on the treacherous trail to save life on earth in order to find the root causes of our human dilemma. We have hiked from Lucy's cave along the trails her children traveled. We were able to do so by following road markers - material evidence found in archeological digs. There were Lucy's bones, her children's tools, firesides, later cave paintings, the fate of the Neanderthals after the Cro Magnons arrived, a pile of bones of a hundred thousand horses in France and the environmental devastation around the Mediterranean Sea. But these road markers were far and between and I had to use my imagination to tell the story in the most plausible way and to draw a conclusion for the desired diagnosis.

We are not on the summit yet, since we are still looking for the source of the other strain we inherited, the genocidal strain, which we called our greatest shame, well documented in prehistory through the disappearance of the Neanderthals and well documented throughout history to this day. In the twentieth century alone man has killed 100 million of his own in world wars and other killings. This is unprecedented in evolutionary history. It begs the question, where does this come from? How can man be so angry, brooding, revengeful, cruel and unpredictably vicious? And how does this go together with man's obvious goodness, his fine achievements and civilization?

Someone might think it's now time for me as a Pastor to talk about good and evil, the topics we believe in while we practice our religion. I remember my surprise when I read the great philosopher of the enlightenment, Immanuel Kant, in his "Critique of practical reason" how he suddenly talked about the "original evil". Few people even know that. Had he not crossed from the realm of philosophy into that of religion? And is there a bridge which allows for such crossing? I didn't think so then, and I don't think so now. I promised you, Professor, to hike with you, and I wanted to do that through the realm of science and philosophy. What is the root cause of our greatest shame, the genocidal/suicidal strain, the weirdness of man, which even tempted a philosopher of Kant's stature to cross the line? Is there a root cause empirically, which allows us to come up with a diagnosis? Let's hike on and find out. It will be a short scramble from here on, steep and with no more markers. Once we are on top however, we will clearly see, where we come from and we will get a strong hint as to where we have to go from here.

In order to answer our puzzling question we have to look at one moment, the most remarkable moment in all of evolution, the day when man appeared on the scene or – to say it bluntly, even crudely: the moment an animal became a human being. It was the day when one individual saw himself or herself for the first time as an "I" and everything else and everyone else became "the other". At that moment the light came on and the reflective/reflexive thinking was born, in other words, this individual had become self-conscious. It was most likely a mutation and spread like wild fire among the tribe and to tribes beyond. I share this opinion with Pierre Teilhard de Chardin, who wrote a very thoughtful chapter on it[13]. Under the title "The Birth of Thinking" he looks carefully at the self-consciousness of the 'I'. The moment when the instinct of a living being saw itself for the first time in the mirror of its own self, the world took a step forward, a step which he compares in its importance with the "condensation" of chemical elements on the early planet and the appearance of life. He is quick to acknowledge that animals can think too, but they do not know that they think.

Of course, evolution had prepared our ancestry for this moment. After they branched off for the last time from the *anthropoids* the *homo sapiens* evolved with larger brains. Larger brains meant larger skulls which led to problems: the size of a baby's skull was limited by the size of the female pelvis through which it had to pass till finally only those babies survived who were born prematurely when the fontanel was still soft and the skull could be somewhat squeezed. This had the added advantage that the brain could still expand after birth but before the child got busy with walking or clinging to the mother's body. It had time to quietly explore and so to shape the brain favorably. For all this there is physiological evidence[14]. But there is no material evidence of the moment when the first individual became self-conscious. Very quietly man came onto the scene, says Teilhard de Chardin, and it seems almost that the universe held its breath in wonder of what was just happening. Elements, atoms of the universe had organized themselves to molecules, cells, and tissue, and now at that glorious moment the universe looked at itself. The spirit was born and from it would flow eventually science and culture, art and religion, all that we treasure as the human expression. The symphony began to play, which I used as a metaphor earlier, the music that would touch the ceiling of the universe and reach for eternity.

However, something else had happened, something dark and potentially deadly. It had already forecast its shadow as a certain weirdness of man had become apparent. Man could change his mind and become unpredictable. While a resting, well fed and full lion is known not to attack, so that a zebra can graze in close range without fear, man had become the exception: you could never know what he could do next. These problems were compounded as soon as he had stepped away and outside the animal kingdom and had recognized himself as an "I' in contrast to all the "others". He became painfully aware of the deep divide between the I and the other, the subject-object divide as philosophy would one day call it[15]. Man did not belong anymore, was no longer embedded in the jungle of life. For him the paradise was lost, and while the party for the "others" seemed to go on, he was not part of it anymore, for there was this nasty divide, which excluded him. On top of this he now recognized his own mortality and struggled with it. He had become utterly lonely and frightened. In him a wound had opened and he would suffer from it for the rest of his life.

I believe that in this wound lies the root cause for what I call the genocidal/suicidal strain in mankind. It is made up of frustration, angst and loneliness[16]. One might call it *the fundamental disturbance of the human soul*. It is a well-known fact that the most horrific crimes are often committed by loners who felt excluded. This is so with fundamentalist and extremist societies who foster terrorism. It is so with the odd student who shoots down his school. For various reasons he had lived isolated. I'm sure the same could be shown to be true for societies and individuals involved in genocides and other crimes against humanity[17]. This leads us to ask how mankind survived for so long. If we carry this wound within us since we came onto the scene why haven't we bled to death a long time ago? The answer is the resilience of man. Facing this nasty divide man went to work immediately to build bridges over this gap, bridges from the "I" to the "other". He wooed the other to come over or allow him to take the first step. Nature had laid the groundwork for this to happen. Of course, males had always chased or wooed females, for obvious reasons. But this bridge building became much more than mere reproduction. Humans needed to hold each other, to feel the heartbeat of another against their own body, for comfort and reassurance that the world would not fall apart. From their first moment, a baby cries for the same reason, "please come and hold me". This bridge building is the act of loving in its simplest form. Culture, art, religion, and philosophy are all acts of bridge building. They all have in common the desire to bridge the gap. Love is the energy driving this desire to build bridges. Man was never without love, but has cried out for it from his first moments. The earliest written texts we have are love songs from Egyptian ostraka or papyri, but long before that, wherever we find signs of human existence, we also find signs of 'bridge building", burial objects, rituals, drawings of animals and other objects. No wonder then that our professor says love is innate. It must be, for it was with us from the very beginning.

While we discussed our own origins, we have now reached the summit and can take a moment to sit down, catch our breath and scan the view we have worked for so hard. From here we can look back and see it all more clearly: man stepping away from the animals via the reflexive thinking, which allows him to gain a view of the whole universe, like God. But he *is* not God, he is still part of the biosphere. Having torn himself away from it he left the biosphere bleeding with trembling fear: what is man going to do now? Where is he going from here? He is bleeding himself from his loneliness and angst. So the hour of evolution's brightest triumph is also the hour of greatest darkness and danger. What is man going to do? If he remains brooding on the rock of his self-consciousness, he will become the most viscious animal the world has seen. He will continue developing what we now euphemistically call the "VIP syndrome of entitlement" or the "I deserve it" attitude. Or man will get off this rock and get to work in an attempt to heal what he has torn apart – stitching himself back into the delicate veil of mother nature's biosphere dress by building bridges from the "I" to the "other" through love and compassion. This will make him human. To become human will forever be a work in progress. In other words we can never stop building these bridges or we continue to be this vicious animal under which all of creation suffers, including ourselves.

What then is this 'bridge building" and how does it work? The shape of these bridges and their capacity to carry are manifold, depending on where they are leading to. Their material is instinct and emotion, enforced by rational thought. We call this package of material love. The amount of rational thought that goes into this structure depends upon how familiar or unfamiliar the object is to the "I". For instance, the love of a mother towards her child comes largely by instinct and emotion. However, the love of one's enemy needs much more initial rational thought to figure out where to anchor the bridge on the enemy's side.

All shapes of these bridges are facets of love; with some of them we are already familiar.
Filia - We've heard of biophilia and Philadelphia,
There is also philanthropy (love of mankind)
Philosophy (love of wisdom) and many more.
Filia is love, which is inclined towards or drawn to or fond of its object.

Compassion - Sympathy – we heard that the Neanderthals had already compassion.

Charity – Charite – Caritas – closely related to the above with emphasis on care and help

Eros - Passionate love of body and/or spirit

Agape - Love of God, the word was coined by the early church in contrast to Eros.

Empathy -

Lets take empathy as an example of how powerful love is and what it can do.

Let's visit Lucy once more on the ground level of the National Museum in Addis Abeba. Lucy is very old. She is 3.18 million years old. She has total dementia. Not a shred of her brain is left. Did I tell you that? No? Did I tell you that she was a bag of bones, even just fragments of bones? I didn't. Instead I showed you how her full lips covered her mouth. You saw her rosy cheeks, her sparkling eyes. Then I counted her ribs. And I showed you her heart, big enough to have room for all her loved ones. We saw her hand shading her eyes from the light. Saw her hand holding her toddler so he would learn to walk upright and free. Her hand luring her man to the back of the cave. I had begun to love this woman. This attitude is empathy. I had given Lucy her life back, made her cheeks rosy again over a gap of more the 3 million years. If I can do this, should we not be able to do the same to our mothers who are still with us and stop saying mom has dementia, is 'a vegetable', has no quality of life? Can we not see that all her life is still within her and increasingly within us? The years she has lived, the love she gave and the love she received.

Her endurance in sacrifice and faithfulness in her work. To see this is to empathize, and empathy preserves dignity and respect.

All these facets of love are innate. They are the potential we are born with, but can only be triggered into action when we get introduced to the other, whether on purpose or by chance. Since we live such a remote lifestyle, isolated from most of nature, we can no longer afford to leave it to chance. We need to be introduced to the other and dates have to be set up. This is what education has to accomplish. To put it provocatively: education has to become more and more a dating service to introduce human beings to their surroundings, and particularly to nature. Only then can filia, charity or any other facet of love become active and the bridge building can begin. Just visualize man sitting on a rock, brooding. A tragic figure, maybe a Greek sculpture or "The Thinker" by Rodin. *Which way will man go?* The consequences of the answer to this question will be enormous and can't be left up to chance anymore. Education has to give the whole picture and lead the student to think. In other words: the dating service has also to become a counseling service and help with the bridge building.

Understandably, love usually makes the strongest impression on us as sexual love. It is not only in mind and soul that we embrace, but also in the body, which provides visible, tangible evidence that we bridged the gap. For a moment the togetherness of paradise seems to be restored, hence our joy and bliss. An embrace does not last, however. This joy and bliss is gone in the flash of a moment. We cannot hang on to it. If a couple decides to stay together for better or for worse, they will begin to build a bridge between them. They will have to realize that the supporting beams or girders have to be made of trust and hope and need to be carefully maintained. Occasionally they might have to undergo a thorough bridge rehabilitation. This is true for any bridge, which is made of love of any facet. (It is of course true for those made of concrete and steel as well) One last thought before we leave the summit.

More often now I hear people say they will only decide what to do with their lives once they have found out *who* they are[18]. This seems to have become a socially accepted or even expected statement. And yet it is wrong: sitting on a rock and gazing at one's own naval might even lead to depression or to the conviction that indeed you are VIP – a very important person.

Of course you are important. But to find out *who* you are you have to seek the "others" and find out who *they* are. *The more you engage with the other the more you become yourself.* Why? Simply because you will learn how interrelated and interdependent we all are, all part of the biosphere, cells of mother nature's delicate skin, part of her filigree veil and most beautiful dress. As part of that you are very important indeed.

With that we conclude our summit. We were able to see the origins of the two strains that threaten the very existence of our species and much of other species as well. It might even be that the strain which I described as "Hunters and Gatherers Unlimited" is not only so powerful through the millions of years of the sequence of repetition and reward, it might even be rooted in the original strain, man's weirdness, his genocidal/suicidal strain, which we saw caused by his loneliness and angst ever since he became self-conscience. The unrestrained hunting and gathering then is an attempt to be noticed and never be forgotten. He ultimately builds himself a legacy, something lasting and for which he can be remembered, like the pyramids of the Egyptian rulers. One of the most famous is the 'Cheops Pyramid', named after one of the Pharaohs[19]. However this might be, at the end of our summit we saw a sign of man's resilience and his goodness, how he tried immediately to remedy his dire situation by building bridges from the "I" to the "others", which I called "to love". This will be the direction in which we have to look as we begin our search for a cure of our ailments.

*Schnepfenthal School
founded by Christian Gotthilf Salzmann in 1785.*

CHAPTER 6

Professor, we have reached an important milestone. By looking back at where we came from we also saw where we will have to go from here. We saw how man reacted to the dilemma he found himself in after he became self-conscious: he began to build bridges. Since the beginning, I said, man was not without love. As we now begin our descent we have to walk carefully so we won't lose anything we found on the summit. But as soon as we have the scramble section behind us – probably when we are safely on the ridge again – I want to have a discussion with you.

I read in your book, Professor, that biophilia, an important facet of the wider spectrum of love, is innate. This makes us, if not singing from the same song sheet, at least sitting in the same section of the band.

In this chapter I will discuss biophilia with you, your concept of education to raise generations of naturalists and finally the call on the Pastor of your childhood and youth to help save life on earth.

ATTEMPTS OF A CURE – A DISCUSSION ON THE RIDGE

Biophilia

While your book "The Creation" is a walk through nature and a ringing of alarm bells to signal that nature is in trouble, at its centre is an attempt to find a solution. You want to help the biosphere, and you pin your hope on biophilia, which you defined earlier as "the innate tendency to affiliate with life and lifelike processes". Biophilia has become an academic discipline, which closely cooperates with conservation in a systematic manner. The human interest in life, or, as you put it metaphorically: "the gravitational pull of nature on the human psyche" can be very useful in conserving life on earth. Biophilia seems to me a dormant energy, which can be triggered and cultivated into a passion for life. However, biophilia is only one facet of love. There are many more. Which is good, for the many facets can address the many more problems we face. Each problem is as deadly as the one we are trying to cure with biophilia. If my analysis is correct – and I can't see it any other way – the universal problem of human development needs a universal approach. Evolution has led mankind into a cul de sac and we cannot get out of it. I called it "the fundamental disturbance of the human psyche". Forever suffering from the wound of the separation of the "I from all the others", we are indeed afflicted - to use a title of a work by Soren Kierkegaard – with the "Sickness unto Death".

But there is hope. It might be that we are in a situation of a man who is being told by the doctor that science can't do anything for him anymore, but if he keeps exercising every day, he can still live a long and full life. You, Professor, pin your hope on biophilia. What I'm saying is: let's not play just on one string, let's play on the whole set of strings, bringing all facets of love into play. Our human exercising must be universally equipped and orchestrated.

So then we – mortally ill as we are – will have to do what man did from the very beginning: build bridges to the "other" but we'll have to do it much more intensely and systematically and collectively: *we will have to steep ourselves in a culture and civilization of love and compassion.* How can we do this? This brings me to the second point I gleaned from your book, your

Concept of education

When I arrived at the pertinent chapters of your book "How to Learn Biophilia and How to Teach It" and "How to Raise a Naturalist" I could not believe my eyes. I had expected the book to peter out by you talking about ants and butterflies. Instead after all your ringing of alarm bells and pinning your hope on biophilia you come up with a concept of education. Professor, my heart began racing when I read this. I had been waiting all my life to meet somebody who would say that even a fundamental problem such as this can be overcome through education, and I am thrilled that I finally have.

Education has been a topic around our family table

quite often. My mother's ancestor had been a renowned educator within the philanthropic movement of the eighteenth century. Christian Gotthilf Salzmann founded a school in 1785, which is still standing and until recently was still in family possession.[20] The place became a Mecca not only for us as a family, but for educators from different countries, predominantly, I believe, from Japan. When winter was over and spring in full bloom, classes at this school were held outdoors. Students and teacher would sit under a tree or on the grass or they would do practical work in gardens or fields. Nature was seen as the best classroom.[21] One of the associate teachers name was GutsMuths. This man found a clearing in a forest nearby and established an open-air gymnastic facility, which was the first one in Germany. Today if you go there you can still see the Double Bar, the Single Bar, the Beam, and the Box. GutsMuths tried to build on the primal instincts of his little boys: swinging between two branches and trying to land safely somewhere else, balancing over a creek on a fallen tree, trying not to slip, jumping over a rock or off a cliff. One of his students was Friedrich Ludwig Jahn. Upon graduation he moved to Berlin, where he organized the first sports association for workers and built a sports facility as he had seen at his school. In less than a hundred years – from the humble beginnings in a forest clearing – a sports movement grew all over Europe, where tracks and fields and gymnasiums were built in every major village or town, which eventually paved the way for the Olympic Games' return. I tell this story only to show what a huge impact educational ideas can have and in what a short time.

You, Professor, gave us your concept of education: start at an early age to give the little toddler the opportunity to unfold the innate biophilia, the passion for life. Then proceed to an introductory education in biology. It is important to note, that after you described "biophilia" you did not stop there, taking comfort that everything will eventually turn out all right, because man is born with love of life. You don't leave it on the individual level or up to chance, you rather lift it to the collective level of public education. As an educator you tell us to teach from the top down, from the general to the specific so as to catch the attention of the students by naming a problem they are familiar with and that's on everyone's mind.

We know the biggest problem that the world has ever faced is the destruction of the biosphere. We know the root causes, those two inherited strains that threaten us. I'm trying to take this problem and its causes and solution in their most comprehensive form to the highest level possible by calling on world leaders for a "Declaration of Love and Compassion". This declaration will name the problem very comprehensively as the prospect of us losing our place on a livable planet, name the causes, and then outline the basic form of a "Charter of Love and Compassion" for individual countries and cultures to adopt. These charters will contain a pledge to take part in a word wide educational enterprise with the goal of reintegrating mankind into the world of the "others" through bridge building. It will undoubtedly result in a new civilization of love and compassion in which we will exercise our humanity for as long as we shall exist.

The call on the Pastor

I'm convinced, Professor, that you are an active bridge builder. I can see you reaching from your lectern over to your young students right where they are – and I know you love them. I imagine you bending down from the height of a tall man over an anthill to study some of the smallest creatures one can see with the naked eye – and I know you love your job. And now we see you reaching out over nearly a lifetime to the Pastor of your youth. With that gesture you span a bridge over three hundred years to the time when science and religion began to drift apart and stopped talking to each other – and we can see how you love your pastor. But why are you talking to him now? Part of the answer might be that you know that believers are supposed to be stewards and caregivers of the planet, for "the earth is God's, and all that is within it". This has become a central doctrine of religion. Another part might be that you know "biophilia" as a facet of love has spiritual qualities and so is an essential building block of our human nature. Churches and religions are sanctuaries and schools of spirituality. This and their mandate to preserve the earth seem to make them your natural allies. But there's even more to it: world religions are by far the largest NGOs in the world. They have immediate access to a majority of the world's population and can communicate not only in the public realm but also in the most private way. Even the mass communication of the media or the internet have not sidelined these organizations, which since ancient times rely on person to person contacts. No surprise then that NGOs, both in the secular and in the religious segments of society become more and more important as the call for a kinder society and a more compassionate world increases. I'm sure, Professor, that your call on the Pastor will not remain unanswered.

Avalanche Valley in Bugaboo Range,
Canadian Rockies

CHAPTER 7

IDEAS

Professor, I'm grateful that we are able to have these discussions. Our summit experience could otherwise be seen as just a lofty and ambitious goal in itself. On our ascent we were driven by urgent questions. Now going down we see from a different perspective. Like on a real hike, the descent is integral part of our hiking experience. It makes us see the landscape from the other side and different angle. You know, Professor, that I share your concern for a livable planet. I pledge my allegiance to your educational concept of alleviating man's estrangement from his surroundings. I will do so by bringing forward a Charter of Love and Compassion. The help of experts from every segment of science, philosophy, art and religion will be needed.

So we take our time. I plan two more stops on our way down. One is opposite an avalanche chute where we will examine the dynamics of a Charter of Love and Compassion. The other stop will be in a clearing of the forest to discuss the concept of "New Charter Schools".

But for now let's enjoy our scenic hike. From our

vantage point so close to the summit we can see our trail clearly. It meanders along the ridge. Then it drops into the basin, passing through sparsely treed meadows, which are covered in daisies. After the meadows the trail drops again and we walk along a placid little lake which is being fed by a melting snowfield. We cross the outlet stream on a tiny bridge. Here originates the creek, which we will follow down to the trail head. At first the creek runs through a wet, marshy area. Lumps of moss, lichens, flowers with tiny blossoms grow beside the trail. Friends of Nature have installed half logs. We balance careful not to disturb the fragile ground with our boots. A marvelous enchanting garden. Soon the trees begin again. We step on solid ground as the dark forest swallows us up. We keep walking. Occasionally we stop and listen to rushing waters, a sign that the creek is not far away. We have now hiked a good half hour, when the forest suddenly comes to an end and we find ourselves on a rocky slope, partially overgrown by shrubs, grass, and flowers. We have arrived at our first stop on the way down.

THE AVALANCHE CHUTE AND THE CHARTER OF LOVE AND COMPASSION

We are now half way across the slope and sit down on some rocks. As we look at the mountainside opposite us we have an avalanche chute in full view. It looks like a green ribbon thrown down the mountain, a carpet glittering with wetness. The green is light and in sharp contrast to the dark trees, which frame the chute on both sides. Avalanche chutes are Mother Nature's way to renew her skin. Snow accumulates below the ridge. It melts and freezes over again. More snow packs it all down till it becomes so heavy that anything can trigger the snow to break loose, a fallen rock or a wind gust. By its sheer weight and speed the avalanche plows the mountain side taking with it trees and rocks, bringing new minerals to the surface and pressing seedlings into the ground. Moisture from melting snow is trickling down all summer. The results are stretches of the most diverse biosphere. A mini jungle of lush plants, herbs, grassed, shrubs, and young trees give shelter to a host of rodents, birds, and insects. Mountain Goats and Bighorn Sheep are feeding on the potent greens. The Grizzly is waiting in the wings of the forest edge for the big kill. Even the Cougar is not far away, prowling in the shade of the upper ridge. All this life is possible through the avalanche event, which happens periodically as nature renews her skin.

Human societies and civilizations are part of the biosphere. They live and they die and from time to time they renew themselves. We call these processes Renaissance or Reform movements. They happen in a similar fashion like avalanche events. Knowledge accumulates over time and sometimes rapidly as it did during the 15th and 16th century. It had begun with the Renaissance in Italy and spread soon to central and northern Europe. When the powers of the day tried to stop the movement and began to prosecute its proponents – some were even burned at the stake[22)]

– the suffering of these early reformers only added weight to the "pack" of knowledge. It was the weight of ideas in human brains. Philosophers might say: it was the weight of truth. Eventually this weight became so overwhelming that a little vibration would be enough to cause the "pack" to slide down and unleash its full power. It happened through an obscure monk of an obscure town in Germany when he nailed 95 theses to a church door[23]. This act triggered the Reformation. Aided by the earlier invention of the printing press [24] the movement swept all over Europe. None of the Reformers was a libertarian, and yet their quest to uncover the truth eventually led to the enlightenment and later the proclamation of the 'Charter of Rights and Freedoms'. This is due to the 'avalanche effect'. We know already avalanches in the mountains are good tools of nature to renew herself. Avalanches of knowledge and truth are good too. Truth will set us free.

As we face unprecedented challenges, new knowledge is being accumulated. The truth once more manifests itself in the human spirit. Once it unleashes its power nobody can predict the extend of change our global society will go through. Only this much we know: it will be good for us. We will become a happier society and less stressed out over our material 'progress'[25].

Like any other reform movement the call for a Charter of Love and Compassion has its forerunners. During the Prague Spring of 1968 Alexander Dubcek tried to give Communism a 'Human Face'. In 1970 and again in 1980 Lech Walesa led a strike movement called Salidarnoc (solidarity) in Poland. Solidarity can be seen as a facet of love or bridge building. The movement continued enjoying the support of a strong Polish Catholic Church and was helped by the fact that Pope John Paul II had hailed from that country. In the Soviet Union Michael Gorbachev surprised the world that his chairmanship would pursue "glasnost and perestroika", transparency and restructuring, buzzwords which became soon known around the world. In former East Germany young people gathered in churches to pray for peace, then walked through the streets with candles in their hands. They were joined by others who week after week walked with them quietly holding their own candles. Soon they numbered in the hundred thousands till the Berlin Wall came down – the greatest event in modern history when the world moved away from the edge of guaranteed mutual annihilation. We must not forget that all this started with acts of bridge building or loving-kindness: trying to give a 'human face' to society, glasnost, solidarnoc, peace prayers. To make this unforgettable clear: in the aftermath of the wall coming down, when the lives of former dictators were in danger, an East German Pastor sheltered the most notorious of those dictators, Erich Honecker, in his parsonage. Love your enemy! The most paradoxical of all commandments. And yet, this was just the culminating point of the much broader movement of bridge building through dialogue and peaceful actions. More recently a movement was started in the Western World by Karen Armstrong[26] who calls for a Charter of Compassion. All these remarkable events and the good will of so many people involved tell me that the time has come to move forward. The discussion has started and will continue in chat rooms, on twitter and face-book, or wherever people congregate. They will ask how we can become a kinder society, or how to unleash the good powers and restrain the predatory ones within us. I believe the truth has its own dynamic, for once it has manifested itself in the human spirit, nothing can stop it. Subsequently a charter of love and compassion, once proclaimed, will run pretty much on its own power, precisely because it is based on truth. Organizations and initiatives will spring up on issues derived from the charter as they have emerged around the Charter of Rights and Freedom. However, we will need a unified and global approach to start the process in earnest.

————————————————————————

Consider that the bodies of world religions are mandated by the United Nations to convene – or they convene on their own initiative – to consider the following questions:

1) Can you agree that loving-kindness/love and compassion are at the centre of your teaching or the ethics derived from such teaching?
2) Can you agree that love and compassion are the highest expression of humanity?
3) Can you envision an educational approach to set free the powers of love and compassion in all its forms in order to subdue the inherited strains, which pull us down and threaten not only our human species but all life on earth?

If such a convention would agree on only *one* of

these questions it would already create a sufficiently large base to proceed from.

The next step would be to set up a Grand Forum, which at its core would involve scientists, researchers, and educators but also artists like writers, singer songwriters, as well as legal advisors and eventually politicians. The Millenium Generation, those born after 1980 and the first ones to have grown up with the computer should have a strong representation[27]. The task of the Grand Forum will be first to come up with a draft resolution for a Charter of Love and Compassion and secondly to produce an educational concept of reintegrating man into the world of the "others".

This new educational concept will be a part of the Charter and is still a way off. We will discuss its possibilities at our next stop at the clearing in the forest. However, there are some measures, which can be taken right away to improve our existing excellent system of Kindergarten, Elementary and High School and College. Here is my wish list:

1) I wish we could train more effectively in critical thinking. For example, multiple choice questions are counter productive as this practice pretends that only one answer is the right one. For a vast array of academic subjects this is not true.

2) I wish that the subject "biosphere/biodiversity – our connectiveness and interdependence with all life on earth" could be taught from Kindergarten on.

3) I also would welcome a new course, which

teaches all facets of love and what impact love can have on human lives.

4) I wish every school could employ a storyteller who travels from classroom to classroom well versed in all sciences as if she came right out of Discovery Channel. She may tell a story of the many lives of a parasite, or the secret memory of our human cells. She may establish with the students our address in the universe or our address in evolution or the biosphere. She may tell about great discoveries in Math and Physics and the stunning careers that young explorers built for themselves. The possibilities are endless.

But let's hike on.

THE CLEARING IN THE FOREST AND THE NEW CHARTER SCHOOLS

We walk for an hour, mostly through forest. Then we turn to the left and follow a deer trail. After a hundred yards we enter the clearing. It is about 60 to 80 feet across and surrounded by high timber. The forest floor is all covered by moss due to a light mist rising from the creek nearby. There is little sunshine reaching the floor. Only a few rays shine through the top of the trees giving the place a cathedral like feeling. I wonder if animals have any sense of the awe, which we feel when we enter this area. Maybe not. Immediately I envision a log cabin standing against the dark trees with a bench in front. It is a place where one wants to stay for a while as if the soul might breeze easier here. We cross the clearing and step unto a rock shield which stretches as an outcropping over the creek below. As we look to the left in the direction where we came from, we can see the summit once more and remember what we recognized there: *the weirdness of man and the fundamental disturbance of the human soul,* but also *his apparent goodness and attempts at bridge building.*

Now we turn our heads and look in the opposite direction. With the help of binoculars we can see a highway in the distance and trucks coming from the border. Down there it is 'business as usual'. We can even make out some human habitations. We are standing in the middle. On the one side the apparent truth, gaining more and more weight like a snow pack below the mountain ridge, on the other side the weight of reality, the hunting and gathering across borders and highways.

We go back to the solitude of the clearing.

If we want to steep ourselves into a culture of love and compassion in order to save life on earth we will have to do it in the real world through education. Our present educational system has to be supplemented by a parallel system of schools for lifelong learning. I call these new schools 'The New Charter Schools'.

STATEMENT OF PURPOSE

The New Charter School will teach love and compassion as means of bridge building in order to reintegrate man into the world of the others.

These new facilities will dot the landscape like

the sports facilities eventually dotted Europe and now the whole world. They will be located away from the heavy traffic of hunting and gathering in places like this clearing in the forest or a medieval monastery or European spa. In order to attend such school one has to travel and stay for a minimum of three weeks. The feasibility of such concept is being demonstrated in Thailand. Each Thai has to stay at a monastery for six weeks before he is recognized as a man. I am not suggesting to build monasteries, or imply any gender restrictions. All these schools, regardless of who sponsors them, will be regulated by a secular Charter of Love and Compassion. Possible sponsors are foundations, charities, governments, or interest groups. These schools will be open to everyone. High school graduates will have to demonstrate that they have taken at least one of the courses. Later in life people can be referred to these schools by their doctor, spiritual adviser, therapist, employer, or by a judge. They can also register on their own. Anyone seeking public office in the broadest sense might be required to have attended at least three times. Upon assuming this office he/she will agree to attend one of the retreats every year.

What will these courses offer?

I cannot prejudge the findings of the Grand Forum. Their experts will design the curriculum. I can only assume that the topics we raised so far will be a significant part of it, such as 'orientation' (where are we coming from etc.), the genetic entrapment of man (hunter and gatherer, genocidal/suicidal man), his goodness and attempt in bridge building, love and compassion in all its forms.[28] Let's not speculate any further.

––––––––––––––––––

New Charter Schools are training centres for person building through bridge building, not to indoctrinate people with ideology but rather decode the potential which is in every human being, or in the words of our Professor: to cultivate our capabilities. While there will be some pointed presentations of knowledge, there will also be wide-open discussions. There will also be sessions of meditation and visualization[29], times of solitude and times of socializing.

––––––––––––––––––––

WHY DO WE NEED A NEW CHARTER

As we now leave the clearing and take the final descent to the trail head I want to explain why I think another Charter is necessary. The problems – as explained – are huge: we are heading towards a meltdown, not only of sea ice but the climate change will put the integrity of the biosphere and the condition of human existence on the planet at risk. Other factors compound the problem.

We hear calls for help. Like your call, Professor. You tell us that biophilia is innate. Neurologists tell us the same about empathy. Behavioral researchers and linguists point out the importance of love and empathy. Everyone understands that little children develop best in a loving environment. All our good intensions however are sidelined by our hectic lifestyles and ambitions. Calls to be nice to each other or the hippie slogan "make love and not war" won't cut it. We have to "cultivate our capabilities" as you, Professor, have said. That means we have to build a Culture of Love and Compassion. For this we need a second charter.

Let me use an analogy. Our human brain has two distinct parts: a left side and a right side. Each side has different functions or seats for different capabilities. If the brain suffers damage, let's say from a stroke, usually one side looses parts of its functions. The person suffers disabilities (cannot walk or cannot talk or see).

The head of our global society is the United Nations. The UN tries to prevent war, fights poverty, calls for equality, tries to regulate environmental protection etc. All these laudable goals are based on the Charter of Rights and Freedoms. There are significant results, and I can't even imagine where we would be without these efforts. And yet we are still drifting with accelerated speed for global disaster. And that is so because we have not developed or cultivated "the other side". Culture and arts for instance are only minimally present in the sub-organization UNESCO. Love and compassion is left up to churches and mosques.

But here is our potential. A second charter will act analogue the other part of the brain. It has to be an organization with its own seat. If it is going to be effective it will have its own powers and structures. The two structures, the UN and the new organization will communicate. The two charters will inform and condition each other. For instance the Charter of Rights and Freedoms makes it impossible that someone is punished for not being kind and loving.

As for the seat of the headquarters of the new organization I consider China the obvious choice, maybe India. Sub-organizations might be located in a Moslem country like Egypt, in Ethiopia, South Africa, and Scandinavia.

––––––––––––––––––––––––––––––

With these 'ideas' we have already gone beyond our mission, have hiked down to the inhabited levels of everyday life. You, Professor, will go back to your studies as I go back to my ministry. But before I do I will draft a manifesto and call for a Charter of Love and Compassion and then say a last word to 'The Man in the Dark Suit'.

Thank you for inviting the Pastor to the dialogue. I was very much privileged to be in your company on issues that concern all of us.

I wish you the very best.

God bless!

MANIFESTO

A call for a

Charter of Love and Compassion

Warnings have been issued that our global society is being threatened by the destruction of the biosphere, by climate change, by scarcity of food and clean water and ensuing pandemics and wars. Some of these warnings have been heard for many decades when it was already clear that the western economies alone left too big a footprint to remain sustainable. With new emerging economies and ever increasing GDPs worldwide the footprint of mankind on nature becomes so big that it will inevitably lead to a global catastrophe and the prospect of an unlivable planet at the end of the century.

However, there is no need to panic.

There is no time for denial.

The human dilemma is an evolutionary one. We have not only emerged as compulsive hunters and gatherers, we are also burdened with a genocidal/suicidal strain within us.

However, we are also born with an ability to reconnect ourselves to the "others". The potential of love and compassion is innate. If we can cultivate these capabilities we will be able to restrain the Hunter and Gatherer and Genocidal/Suicidal Man in us.

We need to retool our civilization so that love and compassion can be cultivated in a systematic and universal manner. This will be done through educational measures. Similar to training our bodies at the gym on an ongoing basis, we will train our inner self at educational training centres.

I call on the Youth of the world to rally for a Charter of Love and Compassion.

Remember it is your future and the future of the children you want to have. Inform yourself. Discuss the issues. Network worldwide on Twitter, Facebook or other sites. We want to retool our civilization in order to move from a consumer society to a society of keepers and caregivers of the earth.

Envision a world where the yardstick for success is no longer the GDP (Gross Domestic Product) but the GDH – Gross Domestic Happiness. Work together with friends. Once you have 10,000 friends you'll take to the streets with your candles in hand. You will see the wall coming down that cuts you off from the future. You will have made evolutionary history.

I call on World Leaders in religion and science, philosophy and education. Join the call for a Charter of Love and Compassion.

Think strategically. We have no time to waste. Network across the disciplines. Design the tools we need to undertake the biggest project of change in human history: to relegate the Hunter and Gatherer and Genocidal/Suicidal Man to the past and open the present to a society of loving-kindness. If we concentrate on the simple truth, the human spirit will be empowered to succeed.

The truth will set us free.

Friedmut Wilhelm

Post Script

The Man in the Dark Suit – "Where are we going"

I barely remember his face: I never learned his name. I met him in Frankfurt. Had I met him before? At soccer parties, in public squares, on sidewalks, in grocery stores and private homes? He loomed large over every chapter I wrote, the Man in the Dark Suit, the reader, whose name I don't know either. He asks me the question 'where are we going?' A question for the Pastor, a fundamentally religious question: is there any meaning of life and where does it all lead to?

I owe it to him and anyone who hears me preach and trusts me for spiritual guidance to answer briefly.

Real orientation begins for me at the parameter of the universe and the parameters of our human life. We come from God and we go to God, all of us and the entire universe. And this not by innate qualities of our own but by the gracious will of a gracious God.

This does not mean that we hope for "eternal hunting grounds" nor for fire and hell and condemnation of the "others". How would anyone want to eternalize an inherited strain, which we managed so poorly, or the fundamental disturbance of the human soul, which created so much hell on earth? None of that!

However the orientation on God is the anchor of my freedom: knowing that we shall not perish like a rotten apple, for the universe is not a random event, I have my hands free to do the work of a caregiver and guardian of the earth.

If there is a good reason that John 3, 16 is such a favorite saying among us, then we can expect that Christians – in fact all believers – will be at the frontline of building a new society under the Charter of Love and Compassion.

References and Notes

---

1) E.O. Wilson, The Creation, An Appeal to Save Life on Earth. W.W. Norton & Co. New York 2006
2) Wilson, Creation, pg. 133
3) Wilson, Creation, pg. 66f
4) Paleontologists came to this conclusion by studying the bones of people crippled by osteoarthritis, who apparently were cared for or would not have survived. See Ronald Wright A Short History of Progress, Anansi, Toronto 2004
5) The time of 1 million year has been arbitrarily set by myself for the purpose of story telling. The latest dating results of Lucy's skeleton is just under 3,18 million years. This makes her the oldest hominid (homo erectus) ever discovered. But as Jared Diamond points out these datings are under constant review and open for significant corrections – see J. Diamond, "Guns, Germs and Steel", pg. 37. In 2009 another skeleton was found in Ethiopia, apparently female too, but much older still.
6) Genesis 10: 8f
7) I owe my information largely to Ronald Wright,

A Short History of Progress– see there: II
The Great Experiment pg. 29ff

8) Of course there were also other factors in these extinctions of big mammals, like climate change, Ice Ages for instance. However, the big slaughter sites speak for themselves.

9) The Mesolithik is a transitional period which some researchers attach to the Upper Paleolithic, others to the early Neolithic. This transitional period occurred on a sliding timescale in different places roughly 9000 – 7000 B.C.

10) See Ronald Wright, Short History IV Pyramid Schemes pg. 99 – 102

11) "The Limits to Growth", a report by the Club of Rome, authored by the Massachusetts Institute of Technology (MIT) Universe Books, New York, 1972

12) While much has been written on the dying of the Coral Reefs also referred to as Coral Bleaching, my reporting is based on an article by Chris Turner "The Age of Breathing Underwater", Walrus Magazine Oct.2009, Toronto, Ontario, Canada

13) Pierre Teilhard de Chardin, La Phénomène humain, Editiones du Seuil

14) Adolf Portmann, Zoologie und das neue Bild des Menschen, Rohwohlt, Hamburg 1956

15) See Friedrich Hegel on the "Subjekt - Objekt Spaltung" in "The Phenomenology of the Spirit"

16) Modern Philosophies have dealt with these subjects albeit from a different   angle. Soren Kierkegaard,

The Sickness unto Death; Albert Camus, The Stranger; Martin Heidegger in Sein und Zeit (Being and Time)

17) Criminal courts deal with these arguments all the time; however, they are not accepted as excuses. The knowledge that loneliness and the feeling of exclusion can lead to horrific crimes is ancient. See the story of Cain and Abel at Genesis 4. Cain fails to connect with his God and out of frustration kills his brother.

18) Existentialism has centered around this question. A more practical introduction can be found in "Oblomov", a novel by Iwan A. Gontscharow.

19) Cheops belonged to the fourth dynasty and reigned about 2530 BC

20) Salzmann's school at Schnepfenthal/Waltershausen, Thuringia, Germany

21) It might interest the entomologist that Salzmann published his ideas under the title: The little Antbook, Das Ameisenbüchlein.

22) Socrates, cup of poison 399 BC, Johann Hus 1415, Savonarola, hanging 1498, Giordano Bruno 1600

23) October 31, 1517 Martin Luther, Castle Church

24) Johann Gutenberg 1453

25) The country of Bhutan replaced the GDP as a measure of progress with the GDH – Gross Domestic Happiness.

26) Karen Armstrong, Twelve Steps to a Compassionate Life, Alfred A. Knopf, New York, Toronto, 2011

27) Frans de Waal "The Age of Empathy", McClelland Steward Ltd., Toronto, Ont. 2010

28) The Millenium Generation has a very different perspective on life than any other generation due to their permanent use of electronic media. We will have to closely listen to them.

29) Love and compassion – love in all its facets is at the centre of the teaching. It must be made clear from the outset that love is a physiological based function and not something mysterious that comes to us from the ether through the arrow of cupid. All aspects of love are bodily functions: my love of my job, of a woman, of the mountains, the water or animals, all love is possible through our *innate ability to attach ourselves to others.* We react to the attractions we feel, to the gravitational pull of others on our psyche. We are not compulsively bound by these attractions. We don't have to "fall" into love; we can walk into it on our free decision or even walk away from it. Happiness and joy is probably felt where attraction and free choice are in the right balance. In any case if love is innate, part of our hereditary rules, encoded in "molecular pathways, cells and tissue" (Wilson, Creation pg.64), then any teaching and attempts to cultivate love has to pay attention to our bodies. We are not used to this in western thinking, where body is traditionally seen as servant of the mind but in fact mind and body are equal partners. See Richard Schusterman Body Consciousness, A Philosophy of Mindfulness and Somaestetics, Univ. Press, Cambridge 2009.

Eastern tradition has long developed methods to unleash the potentials encoded in our bodies through meditation, visualization, breathing techniques or posture. Psychologists are increasingly trained in these techniques, and we can expect important contributions from their side to the teaching at the New Charter Schools.

30) See David Fontana, Creative Meditation and Visualization, Watkins Publishing, London 2007

About the Author

Born in Germany in 1941, Friedmut Wilhelm lost his father to the war shortly after birth and was raised along with three older sisters by his mother in what would become communist East Germany. He studied theology at the Humboldt University in East Berlin in order to become a Lutheran pastor, and attended courses in philosophy, history and art history. He also pursued a childhood interest in paleontology. In the course of his ministry in East Germany and in working for a more humane and compassionate society, he frequently ran into conflicts with the communist authorities. Inspired by the civil rights movement in America, Pastor Wilhelm worked intensively and successfully with the youth, which increasingly irritated the East German regime. In 1979, he accepted a call from a congregation in Western Canada, where he moved with his wife and children and served in a number of congregations.